Part of the "NEARBY" series of books.

THE BACKYARD

Part of the "Nearby" series of books.

BY: DA BUTLER

In a backyard nearby, brothers Arthur and Andy played in their sandbox. Arthur loved to dig with his shovel and fill up his bucket. Andy liked to use his hands. The sun was shining and Arthur and Andy could feel the warmth on their faces. Winter was finally over and spring was here. Now, they can play outside every day.

Arthur and Andy's mom is working in her garden and watches as the boys explore every inch of their sandbox.

"You know boys, there is much more to see in the backyard than just the sandbox," she said.

Arthur and Andy stopped what they were doing and looked around. What else was there? They listened. They couldn't hear anything. They listened again. Suddenly they could hear a strange sound coming from a big tree nearby. What was that funny sound? It sounded like "tap tap tap".

Who else was in the backyard? What could be making that sound? Arthur and Andy started off to find out where the sound was coming from. They couldn't see anything making that "tap tap tap" sound. Arthur and Andy's mom walked over to help the boys find out where the tapping was coming from. As they looked around the backyard the sound got louder and louder. They knew they were about to solve the mystery!

Arthur and Andy looked up and saw a small bird in the tree. They watched as the bird started to peck against the side of the tree, "tap tap tap." "Mommy, look!" the boys squealed. Arthur and Andy's mom looked up and saw a woodpecker happily tapping on their favorite tree.

"Why is he tapping, mommy?" Arthur asked.

"Yes, mommy, why is he doing that?" echoed Andy.

Arthur and Andy's mother explained that woodpeckers tap to find food. "He is looking for ants and other insects in the sap of the tree." The boys jumped in excitement nd danced in a circle chanting "tap tap tap, tap tap tap".

All of the chanting was too loud and their backyard visitor flew away. Arthur and Andy decided to head back to their sandbox. As they were about to step back in to play with their shovels, Andy heard another funny sound!

"What is that squeaking noise?" he asked. Arthur froze and listened carefully.

"Mommy, do you hear that sound?" Mommy listened carefully and heard "squeak, squeak."

Arthur and Andy saw a brown squirrel run across the grass, climb the fence and hop to the nearest branch of the tree. The boys watched as the squirrel climbed high in the tree, then all the way back down. He squeaked once more and hopped back onto the fence.

"Mommy! What is he doing? He looks very busy!"

Arthur and Andy's mom told her boys that squirrels are always very busy. In the spring they gather supplies to make their homes, like bark and twigs. They will look for berries and vegetables, small insects and eggs in the spring. When the fall comes they will gather nuts, like acorns and walnuts. They gather nuts and hide them so they can eat during the winter.

The squirrel took one last look at Arthur and Andy, let out a squeak and ran out of their backyard. As the boys headed towards their house with their mom, they couldn't stop talking about the woodpecker and the squirrel. They were very excited to learn about them.

Mommy asked the boys if they wanted to help her in the garden. Arthur and Andy knew that digging in the dirt was fun, so they grabbed their shovels and walked over to help. Arthur started helping his mom but Andy noticed something out of the corner of his eye and went to investigate.

"Arthur, come and see!" Andy was very excited to see a small, red insect crawling in the garden. Arthur bent down beside Andy to get a closer look.

"Mom, what is this?" Andy asked. "I've never seen a bug like this before." Andy's mom walked over to take a look.

"That's a ladybug, isn't she pretty!"

Ladybugs are very useful in the garden. They eat a lot of other bugs that harm my plants, which helps my plants and vegetables grow."

Mom added, "do you boys know that one ladybug can eat up to 5,000 insects in their lifetime, that's a lot of bugs!"

Arthur and Andy were so happy that they had looked around their backyard today. There were so many interesting and fun things to see and learn about. Today they saw a woodpecker, a squirrel and a ladybug. What will they find tomorrow? What can you see in your backyard?

Arthur and Andy can't wait to go on their next adventure, where will they visit next?

More titles in the NEARBY series:

The Fire Station
The Farm
The Library

Other DA BUTLER titles:

My Glasses
Freckles!
My Daddy
Kindness
Forever Friend
The New Baby

www.ingramcontent.com/pod-product-compliance
Lightning Source LLC
Chambersburg PA
CBHW041404010526
44107CB00015B/1068